for some
great friends —
un abrazo
de Leroy y Yolanda

Junio 21/1981

Española,
Nuevo Mejico

Buena
Suerte

SANGRE

Leroy V. Quintana

PRIMA AGUA PRESS
LAS CRUCES, NEW MEXICO

Some poems published or forthcoming in the following magazines or anthologies: New Mexico Magazine, New Mexico Humanities Review, River Sedge, The Greenfield Review, Tejidos, Colorado State Review, Nuestro, River Styx, Phantasm, Descant, New America, Poetry Texas, A Geography of Poets, 101 Poets of the 60's and 70's, The San Marcos Review, English in Texas, The Indian Rio Grande, Contact II, La Confluencia, Voices from the Rio Grande.

Published by Prima Agua Press
302 Union
Las Cruces, New Mexico 88001

para Sandra

… a ghostly race
Who still ply in my body their mysterious
Disciplines, habits, and anxieties.
Shadowy as if they had never been …

Borges

I

SANGRE 1

Grandma was a Sánchez, her birth certificate
destroyed in a fire long, long ago.
There is only one story about her
in the family: Once, during Lent,
the shrill whistle of the Penitentes
in the nearby hills, she lay in bed asleep
when a strange feeling came over her
in her dreams and caused her to awaken;
she tried to call to grandfather for help
but could not, was paralyzed by the sight
of a shadow of a cadaver on the wall
as it moved across the window
in the light of the full moon.

The rest is only the mention
of how hard she worked all her life
and how sick she always was.

Her blood flows through the family tree
as simple and quiet as stones.

SANGRE 2

In the summertime
Grandmother would sit outside
in the evening, puffing
on her brown paper cigarrito

and tell me about the virhuela epidemic
of her childhood, show me
three or four marks on her arm

explain their resemblance
to some constellation in the heavens
each star was a child in her family
her mother told her as a girl

Grandmother was the large star
a large pock mark
the one who survived

SANGRE 3

There are many stories in the family
about grandfather:

It is said that as a youth he was so strong
it took two men to take him down.

In his time he walked to Wyoming to shear sheep
so many times he couldn't remember how many.

He never had shoes as a young shepherd boy
because his parents couldn't afford any,
he cut his feet on the rocks
when he walked the hills
looking for stray lambs.
Many years later, in a V.A. hospital
said he could hear the saw
cutting through the bone
when his leg was amputated.
Never said anything about the other leg
after it was severed.

When he was a fletero,
carrying different types of freight
in his carro de caballos,
he spent one night, perhaps his longest,
in a room of a casa despoblada
frozen with fear, as a group of brujas danced,
he saw their shadows on the walls
flickering like the flames
of the candles in the next room
back and forth, back and forth, until dawn.

These stories about grandpa have been told
in the rooms of my family's homes
across the years, while the brujas
of our haunted blood dance
in the next room, dance in the next room.

SANGRE 4

Grandfather had a little brother, Enrique,
who walked with him all the way to Wyoming
to shear sheep and never returned.

According to the story, on their way home
they stopped at a bar in Pueblo
and young Enrique, not used to drinking,
downed one shot of whiskey after another,
despite grandfather's words of caution,
continued downing whiskey after whiskey,
and when grandfather said they
had to be on their way, Enrique refused,
ignored grandfather's pleas, and finally,
after more pleading and arguing,
grandfather decided, against his own will,
to continue the journey home alone.

Grandfather's arrival at home was met with tears,
a telegraph from Pueblo stating Enrique was dead.
In time grandfather would learn Enrique had been
beaten to death, his body placed on the railroad tracks
to make it appear as if he had stumbled, fallen
on them in a drunken stupor, but strangely,
no trains had passed through Pueblo that night.
Enrique was identified by others on their way home
from the sheep ranches, perhaps the very men
who had murdered him for his money.

The telegraph had also served notice that Enrique
was to be buried in three days, according to the law,
and grandfather had to decide between returning
to Pueblo to claim the body, and spending the Wyoming money,
that would feed his family until the next shearing season,
to have the body sent home by train for a proper burial.

I am told grandfather was filled with regret
over the fact he did not go back,
and was haunted for the rest of his days,
knowing he had left Enrique behind, and alone
forever somewhere in a potter's field in Pueblo.

SANGRE 5

It is said that one of grandma's aunts was a bruja.
One day she went to grandma's house for a visit
and after drinking coffee and talking
she said goodbye and started towards the door
but only got as far as the sheepskin rug
under which grandma had placed two crossed needles.
She made an excuse not to leave,
returned to her chair, had more coffee, and talked.

A while later she said it was getting late,
said goodbye again, but again
only got as far as the rug, hesitated,
said to grandma that perhaps
they should talk some more, they did,
and drank more coffee, then she said goodbye again,
but still could go no further than the rug
and finally she asked grandma to remove
the crossed needles, which grandma did.

Her blood is a mystery
flowing step by hesitating step
through the family tree,
never stepping over the crossed needles
to walk out the door—
defying us to tell
how she ever walked in.

SANGRE 6

One of grandfather's brothers
carved their father's tombstone
out of a block of stone.

It took him several years,
cutting and chipping,
etching curlicues
and finally, polishing.

It stands in the camposanto in Barney,
a cross, with the name and dates:

    EUGENIO JIRON
    1850 - 1927

Everybody in that part of the world
said that tombstone was the most beautiful
in the camposanto, the condao.

And when grandfather's brother passed away
people came to pay their respects;
they said that man was a man of great patience;
one who could do great things with his hands

and could've made a lot of money
if he had chosen to carve stone
instead of taking care of his father's rancho.

SANGRE 7

Grandma would tell a tale about an uncle
of hers, a vaquero, expert with a lazo,
who bought a brand new pair of boots once,
was so proud of them, the good leather
and the large heels perfect for killing
víboras. You see, he loved to kill víboras.

He would corner a víbora, tease it
with a long stick until it would tire,
then grab it by the tail, twirl it
over his head swiftly the way he did his lazo,
then beat it against the ground several times.

After that he would put his big boot heel
to the víbora's head, drive it into the ground
with all his weight and at the same time
pull back with all his might,
severing the víbora in two. He killed many, many
víboras that way, according to grandma.

He wore those boots for a long time, years,
grandma explained, and little by little
the heels became smaller and smaller.
Time passed, everybody warned him, pleaded with him
not to go on killing víboras, but he wouldn't listen,
refused to replace the old heels,

After all, there wasn't a víbora he couldn't kill.
So he went on killing any that were unlucky
enough to wind their way across his path.
Until one day. One day, one, and it must've been
a large one, a large one bit him,
sank its big fangs through the time-worn heel.

They found him out in the llano a few days later,
grandma would say, her eyes becoming moist
every time she finished that story.
She would stare far far away, puff on her cigarrito,
shake her head slowly, sadly
as that stubborn vaquero's heels wore thinner, thinner.

SANGRE 8

Grandma liked to tell the story about a dog
she had when she was young.
He was so full of mischief, "Era tan traviezo,"
she would say. But that little dog
saved her life more than once.

Grandma lived on a rancho
and there were many many víboras out there.
Whenever she came across a víbora
that dog would draw its attention, corner it,
and fight until he killed it.
He was bitten many times
and the bites would swell into large balls.

But grandma had a way of curing him.
According to her, she'd pour a bucket
of cold well water on him.
The instant the water hit his wounds
they would burst and the poison would run
like thick pus down his sides or legs.
then one more bucketful of water to cleanse him
and he'd scurry into the llano
to let the wounds heal. He'd return
in a few days, as healthy and traviezo as ever.

One day they came across a víbora.
The dog protected grandma,
and, as usual, was bitten.
Grandma carried him home,
threw a bucket of water on him
and he scampered into the llano.
Grandma never saw him again.

He had probably run into another víbora,
was bitten again. He had been bitten so many times
and was so weak he couldn't make it home to die.

Grandma never could figure out how that dog
didn't die a long time before that.
He was so strong, maybe that's what saved him.
It could've been luck,
the fact that he was so traviezo, she'd say,
perhaps it was something in his blood.

SANGRE 9

Grandma was very fond of her brother
a vaquero who was very good with a lazo;
he could spin a loop at his side
or parallel to the ground
and jump through it all day.
He could rope anything with his lazo.
Anything.

But the other women of the family didn't like him,
even though they were fascinated
by the tales of his lazo.
They thought it strange
for a man to spend so much time
in the kitchen talking to them,
and always complained that he
never let them get their work done.

His blood spins strangely
through the lazos of the family tree;
he is the one who jumps in and out
of the odd loops of our veins.

SANGRE 10

You know, it was hard
for the old people
to lose the old ways

When grandma's brother retired
and his government check
came in every month

he decided to become modern
put in a toilet with plumbing
so he bought the pipes and fixtures

and paid the plumbers to install them
but he built the bathroom *outside* the house
only a short walk, not quite as far away

as outhouses in the old days
and with a concrete sidewalk
that led right up to the door

SANGRE 11

There is mention now and then
of one of grandfather's brothers.
Little is known about him,
his strange and silent blood
took him to Colorado
and he has never been heard from since.
This is mentioned now and then,
mentioned among our strange and silent stories.

SANGRE 12

One of grandmother's sons
is said to have seen the devil
on one of those nights long ago
when he, the son, rode his horse home
from a baile somewhere in the hills—
not once, but several times
the devil was always there,
at the place where two roads crossed.

This is one of the stories
in my family; all the older people
swear it is true, swear and tell
and retell this small legend of ours—
except for my uncle who saw the devil,
his blood flows quietly
through the family tree, unlike the rest
whose blood races madly through their veins
like the thundering of hooves at night
long ago, somewhere after the crossroads,
heading home.

SANGRE 13

Grandmother's second son is of fiery and fiendish blood,
a quick-witted and far-sighted man, but infuriated.

He ran for a minor office in his small town
with a vision of a better world, but lost.

He didn't know the evil tricks of the político,
like buying spoiling meat at half price
and placing it on the tables of hungry voters.

This was his first and last venture into politics.
The world and everybody in it
has been going to the devil ever since.

He will recount the times he rode home from a baile,
the nights when he saw the devil at the crossroads.
Swears boldly he saw the devil at the crossroads,
Swears by the devil.

Once, there were old people
who came to grandfather's house
to pay their respects

they would talk about the weather,
how much it had changed
in the last five or six years

it was due to the new bombs
that were being exploded
in the atmosphere, they said

it was getting harder
for a man to make anything grow

their talk sounded as if
they were discussing the ranchos
they once owned and lost,

instead of the small plots of corn
they farmed in their back yards

EULOGIO

Gusanos in his brain, the story went.
Everybody claimed he had gusanos
growing in his brain. Suromato
the small Spanish-American town called him.

Owned the grocery store and grew marijuana
across the alley where grandmother sent me
with cinco centavos now and then
to buy her favorite Golden Grain tabaco.

He had a calendar from Mexico hanging
on the wall. On it was a picture of a rico
in the garden of his hacienda.
A woman was tied to the large tree in the center
and the rico was using a whip on her.
He was dressed in a charro outfit
with studded silver buttons and she wore
a long, sequined skirt with a torn blouse
of blue and blood as bright as the red of Sundays.
A large scarlet flower blossomed
at the tip of one breast. In the background,
a group of men watched and smoked noble thin cigars.
Marijuana in his garden, gusanos in his brain.

Eulogio hardly spoke to his customers
except to ask what they wanted and tell them the cost
after totaling the amount on the cash register.
According to the stories, he grew his plants
in his garden. Another story said he cultivated
his plants in coffee cans kept inside his house.
Gusanos crawling in his brain. Gusanos.

In the evening while Grandmother told cuentos
tales of tesoro, the hanging of Black Jack Ketchum,
of the evil Eulogio and his marijuana, I could see him
watering his squash, carrying coffee cans, the gusanos
eating away at his brain at that very moment
according to the story everybody swore was true, or else
was mitote meant to be told in front of children
Eulogio stooping here and there, picking a few weeds
looking for gusanos.

DESCOJA

> Note: "Descoja" is the formal usage
> of the verb "descojer" —to choose,
> but it is very close to
> "(usted) es coja" or
> "(you) are lame/crippled,"
> especially if the "d" is not
> pronounced very strongly.

In the old days, people recited versos at bailes.
A man could recite a poem to a woman
and win her heart, if he were clever enough.

Of course not all the versos were about love.
Once, a man went to a baile
and saw a woman he disliked very much,
for one reason or another,
perhaps she had spread some mitote about him.
The woman was coja
and sometime during the dance
the man walked up to her
and held out both hands
as if he were asking her to dance
and recited a verse
that asked her to choose
between a flower he held in one hand
and the rose in the other:

> "De esta flor
> Y de esta rosa,
>
> Usted, señorita
> Descoja."

According to my mother,
sometimes the bailes ended early
because of the big fights
caused by the versos.

DON CASIMIRO

A kind man, as I remember him
widower with several sons
vecino who lived across the street
sat in his porch on summer evenings
thinking, looking at the last light of day
fade strangely, fall into a groping darkness.

Grandfather called him "el hombre tuerto"
the one-eyed man, yet he one day showed us
down the back roads of the county
the ranchos that sold good lambs for slaughter.

Grandfather bartered and bought one that day
one that would have a lot of meat
whose hide he could turn into a bedroom rug.

On the way home, as Don Casimiro made fast cigarritos
out of paper and prince albert, they talked
about the old days, a time neither of them
would ever see again.

Once home, grandfather ran a large knife
across the lamb's throat as we held it down
he said to Don Casimiro that lambs never
made a sound when they were slaughtered.

Don Casimiro, I'm sure, knew that
He said that was the way they were
described in the Bible
so I guess he was a religious man too.

His sons took advantage of the fact
he had only one eye to keep on them
they gave up the old ways, saw nothing
in the past, became pachucos, spent
their lives as lions in the poolhall downtown.

II

SANGRE 14

STERLING, COLORADO

"On Saturdays we would go to town
after picking potatoes all week
and the Anglos would laugh at us
and call us dirty Mexicans,"
my mother tells me

as she sits and crochets
surrounded by the red, white, and blue ribbons
won at the State Fair

A picture of John F. Kennedy
smiles from the wall

Her busy, brown hands
pull pulling the thread
from the spool on her carpet

A portrait of Jesus
stares from the wall

The needle flick flick flickering
as she loops the laughter
and pulls the thread, pulls the thread
and she loops the Saturdays
and pulls and pulls the thread
as she loops and loops the laughter
and Saturdays in Sterling
into yet another doilie

SANGRE 15

GRANDMA'S PRIMO

Grandma had a cousin
who lived in the big city
and looked like a gringo

He smoked a big cigar
and spoke English as well
as he spoke Spanish

He loved to tell jokes
would always tell them twice—
the first time in Spanish
to make us laugh
and the second time in English
to impress us

COMO LOS GRINGOS QUE SABEN HABLAR INGLES DESDE CHIQUITOS

The old people had a humorous way
of dealing with youngsters
who thought they knew too much
and began offering their advice freely.

The elders would acknowledge
how smart that youngster was.
So smart indeed! Just as smart
as the Gringos

who knew how to speak English
from the time they were little children.

DOÑA CRUZITA

Doña Cruzita's face was covered with lunares.
And full of lines.
Every year for Christmas,
and I could never understand why,
she would give me a set of Chinese Checkers—
the endless dots and lines
exactly like the riddle of her face.

SANGRE 16

I never knew where he came from
or how his blood was tied to mine—
only that sometimes on Saturdays
he would come up the dirt road
pushed by the idiot boy with the confused smile
the wheelchair rocking from side to side
as it rolled over the stones and through the ruts—
grandma's nephew with the withered limbs.

He is or was the one who painted statues of saints
by holding the brush in his teeth, sold them;
who played his harmonica downtown, at the racetrack
for coins thrown into a cigarbox
the idiot boy placed at his twisted, stockinged feet.

The one who always came with kind words,
a smile for us, the only family he had.
But his life, his room somewhere was always a mystery.
There were stories about his evil moods
taken out on the idiot boy,
and about his drinking, his cursing
the crowds that finally stopped throwing coins
into the cigarbox.

MYRNA

Everybody called her Minnie Mooch, that was her name,
the only name she ever had. To my knowledge
the only Anglo who lived on our side of town.
Wore men's coveralls and shirts, a sunbonnet
over her golden hair, a few stray strands
falling over her ruddy, manly face
the same way strands of mustache
drooped over her unpainted upper lip.

Lived by herself in a shack. Nobody knew
if she had a family. People said she had plenty of money,
but never spent it, kept it hidden in her house,
buried in a corner or under a mattress, if she had one.
Many claimed she had rich relatives in the East.

All the children and so many of the older people
teased her as she walked down the street
Minnie Mooch! Minnie Mooch! Minnie Mooch!
Minnie in her big brogans,
Minnie with a tall shepherd's staff and a large brown bag
Minnie going shopping for groceries in the garbage cans.

DON JOSÉ

As he rolled his cigarrito
Don José would tell a tale
about a man he knew once
named Don Ricardo, I believe

It was a tale of what becomes
of impatience, and of pride

    "Don Ricardo was a proud man,
    the kind who would not give
    los buenas dias to anybody

    One day Don Ricardo was rolling a cigarrito
    when a gust of wind came up
    and blew the tabaco off the paper

    Don Ricardo poured more tabaco on the paper
    and again the wind swept it away

    Don Ricardo tried again, but this time
    the wind took the tabaco
    before it reached the paper
    so Don Ricardo got very angry
    opened the mouth of the bag all the way
    and threw all the tabaco out
    shouting to the wind
    ¡Toma cabrón! ¡Querías tabaco, llévate lo todo!

    And now, because of his impatience
    Don Ricardo no longer had any tabaco
    but he still had the urge to smoke."

"A man," Don José said, and puffed on his cigarrito,
"has to learn to be patient,
or else, like Don Ricardo,
he will have to walk around,
asking people for tabaco."

Not only was the Reyes family different
as far as looks were concerned—
they all had red hair and freckles
but the way grandpa shook his head
when he talked about the father, Don Ricardo
you would've thought that man
was the most worthless man on earth
and all his family a big bunch of big mocosos

all because they were Republicanos,
voted that way every election
even though they lived like we did

EL FIFO

El FiFo strolled through the barrio
as casual as a cat walks a fence,
cautious eyes that stared straight ahead
when we passed;
was only a few inches taller than us
when we were in the seventh grade
his hair slick and shiny
a thousand curls always in place
but we nevertheless feared him
even though the older pachucos
said he gave himself a home permanent
every week.

EMETERIO

All my young life
I saw him
spend his life
walking
to and from the bar
(Sundays to the bootlegger's)

Every morning
in his big, black hat
like Hopalong's,
a pair of pressed overalls
once blue
and then grey and faded
(as his face)

a green khaki shirt
(his mother ironed)
always starched, buttoned
to his Adam's apple

that never worked
a word
out of his throat
unless it was a matter of wine

Drank only tokay,
many times muscatel
and many more pints of port

His hands, smooth as glass,
never knew a woman, warm
and his, (of course,
had cupped his palms
countless times around a bottle
of Virginia Dare,
her breasts)

Every evening
stumbled home, crushed
Cassidy hat and
coveralls wet,
full of wrinkles

the only smiles,
wounds,
he ever
wore.

El Señor Sena was a skinny vecino
who lived across the street
so skinny he looked undernourished
people said "Es porque el Señor Sena
pero no almuerza."

WHERE IN THE HELL WALDO, THE WINO

was talking one day about the time
his wife gave him $5
to fill up the car
and how he used
that money to get drunk.

"You see," he said,
"all I did was open the trunk
and disconnect that little wire
that's hooked to the gas tank.
When it's taken off
the needle on the dashboard
moves to Full and stays there."

He drove to the gas station
put in $1 worth of regular
then drove to the bar
and bought enough pints
of La Copita to stay drunk
for a week, drove home,
and stayed drunk for a week.

His wife was so happy
when she saw that her Waldo
had used all the money
for gas instead of tokay.

And she was so pleased
with the brand of gas
he had put in.
"¡Qué bárbaro!" she said,
"the needle doesn't move from Full!"

But she couldn't understand
where in the Hell Waldo
got the money to get drunk
she checked his pockets twice
every night, her purse three times
and remained utterly puzzled
until she ran out of gas
and had to walk home
and demand where in the hell

ESPIC AND ESPAN

When Estela would talk
with the other women
of the neighborhood
about cleaning house
she always said
her house was espic and espan
because that's what she used—
and recommended

ALFONSO

All Alfonso did
day after day after day after day
was sit on the block fence
(everybody said his ass was flat)
in front of his house

Once he told me
about the death of his son
died a terrible death, crushed
in an automobile accident
even the change in his pocket
was flattened

Another time
when a fat woman walked by
said he loved fat women
(he himself a bit skinny)
because the lips of their cunts
were like big bananas

Those are the only things
of any importance
I can ever remember him saying

And one more fact
Alfonso looked a lot
like Groucho Marx
in Chicano

JUAN Y BARTOLA

i

Both Juan and Bartola
are somewhere in their sixties.
Juan is very hard of hearing.
Bartola has had a throat operation
but somehow manages to shout loud
enough for Juan to hear her.

"If I don't shout he doesn't hear me,"
she says, "I ask him one thing
and he answers another."

"The other day I was telling him something
when the gringo neighbor across the street
came out of his house and began shouting at me:
'What are you, a Women's Libber?
Why don't you leave that poor man alone?' "

ii

Sometimes when you speak to Juan
he'll say "Oiga, yo no oigo."
And sometimes he doesn't.

iii

The other day Juan bought a brand new hearing aid.
"The best," says Bartola, "now he can hear everything
I say. I don't have to shout. When he goes outdoors
he can hear the traffic." "He can even pick up
all the CB channels," she adds, and winks her eye.

iv

"But Juan can't take too much noise,
it makes him nervous. After a while
he has to turn the hearing aid off."

v

Before each dance
Juan asks Bartola
"¿Qué es, Bartola?
¿Qué es?"
"Polka," she'll say,
and Juan dances
the polka with her—
in perfect time
to the silence or
to the music.

NOT EVEN CATS

Bartola was talking about making tamales once
and she remembered the lady who made the masa
in the large tin tub where everybody bathed;
and then told the story about another lady
who walked the barrio selling tamales
and always carried the last dozen in a paper bag
under her arm, "to keep them warm, I suppose,"
chuckled Bartola and then went on to say
she had heard that in Palomas they killed the dogs
and used the meat for their tamales.
"And it must be true," she added,
"if you go there you never see any dogs in the streets.
Ni gatos."

LA LA LA

I never knew
what her name was
just that they
called her La La—
and when referring
to her
la La La

PROCOPIO

Procopio wore a cowboy hat
and boots and thought
he was quite dashing
with his handlebar mustache
was hopelessly in love with Maria Felix
the Mexican screenstar, talked
about being able to make her a happy woman
said he was still fast enough at fifty-five
to chase the young girls
and make them happy too
but one day mentioned the trip
he took to the Santuario, said
he was going forty, imagine! ¡cuarenta!
when all of a sudden his brother
passed him like a bolt of lightning
¡Como un rayo! Que hombre tan loco
that brother of his
drove like a maniac

SANGRE 17

Whenever those of us from the big city
went to visit my aunt and uncle
in their small town
and her relatives came by
there would be the traditional greetings.
After that, her family always felt
they had to speak to us in English,
would ask "When did yous came?"

We always said one half of their English
was from Brooklyn.
The other half, that was down home, mano.
Puro Mejicano.

ENTRE LAS NIEVES

Pablo was very dark, skinny
and not very good looking.
His wife's name was Nieves.
She was light and very fat.

All the men always joked about that,
said they wondered what Pablo
must've looked like
entre las nieves.

DON ENRIQUE'S ADVICE

Don Enrique's advice is very simple.
If you're having a hard time at work
and the patrón is making you miserable
he'll tell you a story of an old sheepherder
whose patrón did nothing but complain
about his work, even though he did it well.

Day in and day out that patrón complained,
resongar y resongar. Nobody could figure out
how or why the old sheepherder put up with it
until one day somebody asked him
and the sheepherder said
he just let the patrón complain and complain

it didn't bother him one bit
because on payday all those resongaderas
turned into pesos.

EL PITO

"Cabrones Mejicanos," Pito would say
after another day of work at the Pizza Palace,
"here we've been making tortillas for centuries
and it never occurred to us
to throw some tomato sauce and queso
on top of one tortilla and call it pizza
or chinga tu madre or anything else
and make a fortune like the Italiano,
I swear I think que Dios laid a curse on us."

POEM FOR PEDRO INFANTE

Today when I heard your voice
in that Mexican bar downtown
I found myself back in grandfather's house
listening to you on those large 78 R.P.M. records
and I wanted to put quarters in the juke box
all day long to listen to you over and over
on that old victrola of grandmother's
that I had to wind every four or five songs

SANGRE 18

At 33
I realized the cross
I've been carrying
was given to me
in a catechism class
when the nuns taught
me to be like God and
turn the other cheek
when they slapped me
treated me with contempt
and mocked my make believe
motorcycle jacket
and bright blue denim pants
idea of me
they must've seen through
and then turned me over
to the world that
cast lots for me

Sister Concepta, Sister of Charity, taught Algebra,
but had no conception of me and very little charity.

There was no equation then, certainly none I knew,
that would make any sense of my mexican life to me.

To her I might've been this: If one term is +
and a similar term is − , the result is zero.

Example:
    $3ab - 3ab = 0$

Reduced to lowest terms, she cancelled me out
of any of her equations of Algebra and Heaven.

To me she will always be a problem, as I suppose I was
to her, each with the term − c involved.

Her − c stood for less chicano,
mine for minus charity.

THEOREM

Perhaps I should've listened
in Plane Geometry
(instead of reading poetry)
until I got caught
and learned an acute angle:
pretend

If I had listened perhaps
today I'd be able to figure out
what type of triangle I can be:
with one obtuse angle Chicano
and another a right angle:
American

black coals from the nearby mines
were the only gems those people
of that small town of my youth
ever knew

they walked to church every sunday
a few went in old pick-up trucks
and prayed

they fasted more during lent,
died with christ for three hours
and rejoiced on easter sunday;
welcomed him every year at christmas,
made sure their children were
baptized, confirmed, made their
first holy communion; and put pennies
in the collection box every sunday
and holy day of obligation

the pastor blessed them, married them
buried them when they died
and bought himself a new car every year

SANGRE 19

PIÑONES

When I was young
we would sit
in front of an old firewood stove
watching grandmother make candy
listening to the abuelos' tales of tesoro,
cuentos of brujería, La Llorona, stories
of the virhuela epidemic, of ranchos long ago—
and eat piñones

Now we belong
to a supersonic age
and have college degrees,
we sit in front of color T.V.'s
watching the Super Bowl
listening to Howard Cosell
stories of riots, wars, inflation, overpopulation—
and eat piñones

In the name of the Father
we prayed, and of the Son
and of the Holy Spirit
and I remember we prayed
first thing in the A.M.
the Angelus at noon
and the last thing
before going home.

We prayed at Christmas,
Lent, and Easter
and all the Holy Days.

We prayed for the Pope,
the Souls in Purgatory,
and for Peace.

And we prayed for
Mother Seton
to be canonized.

But I never prayed
until that day
in Viet Nam

when death walked by
(saw his sallow face,
the slanted eyes)

prayed so hard
the nuns would've prayed
for me to be

the first Chicano
to be canonized
Amen.

i

Eight years after Viet Nam
I still walk the jungles in camouflage
my M-16 mind
on recon patrol
on city streets,
in restaurants, bars, buses,
during breakfast, at work,
morning noon and night,
neighbors, relatives and friends, everybody
even my family
all have slant eyes
I watch their movements
listen to their words
record everything in notebooks

ii

Nine years after Viet Nam
where friendly woodchoppers by day
would be Viet Cong by night
I'm still on recon patrol.
Everybody has slant eyes.
It's an M-16 world.

Teacher by day, tonight
I'm at the trigger
of an electric typewriter.
This paper has yellow skin.
This poem has slant eyes.

Once I knew what numbers were
and what love was.
Once there was a girl
and once there were flowers
and once I picked all their petals
wondering if she loved me
she loved me not
if she loved me:
If you want a girl
to love you begin with "She loves me"
on a flower with an odd number of petals
and with "She loves me not" on a flower
with an even number.
So much for love.
And then I failed at Arithmetic too. And ever since
then it seems I've learned nothing more
about numbers and only a little less about love.

SANGRE 20

Once pain had a purpose
but that was when the world was young
and I dreamed a daydream of me
climbing into the ring to wrestle
for the Heavyweight Championship
of the World, in two out of three falls.

I had learned to endure pain.
Anytime I bumped my head,
an elbow, bruised a finger,
tripped and fell, I told myself
"You have to learn to take it,
that's the way it's going to be
in the ring: the Half-Nelsons,
Step Over Toe Hold, the Crab,
the Turnbuckle Slam, the Flying Mare."

And then one day I read
In Reader's Digest about the phony blows,
the fake falls, the capsules filled
with what was supposed to be blood
and there was no more purpose to pain
whenever somebody stepped on my toe
or I shut a door on my fingers.
No more purpose to pain.

And now, many many years later
I find I am still learning to endure
pain, find a purpose in it:
the Full Nelsons
and Spinning Toe Holds
of these words.

SANGRE 21

Grandfather had a sister, Isabelita,
who is said to have been very beautiful.
A poet composed these lines for her:

    Las muchachas de Clayton
    las traigo en el corazón

    Parece un granito de oro
    la Isabelita Jirón

Nothing else is known or said about her,
except for those versos composed by a poet
and these lines that tie her to a fool

SANGRE 22

A FAIRY TALE

Bedtime. I tell stories, tales
of Robert Rattlesnake, Bennie Beaver,
Yolanda Panda Bear, Jerry Giraffe
and Danny the Dog.
And then it's Elisa's turn. She begins
"Once upanza time......"
"¡Panza!" I say. "It's not upanza,
it's *once upon* a time. This is a panza,"
and grab her stomach, tickle her
until she can laugh no more.
"Once upanza time......"
"No No No No No!" I scream,
"It's *once upon* a time, not *upanza time*."
This is a panza," and I grab her stomach,
tickle her again until she's weak from laughter.
"Please tell me a real story," I plead,
"and please don't say panza."
"Once upanza time ..." she begins.
"O.K.," I say, resigned. "You can say panza."
"Once upanza time
there lived a panza
and it lived happily ever after.
Good night, Daddy."

SANGRE 23

A Poem for Sandra

My little daughter
too soon the teeth of time

will tear you away from me.
I feel so old tonight

three times my thirty three years,
and wiser and richer than any man

when I held the two front teeth
in my palm under the light of the lamp

those gems you lost so proudly today
something of Mother of Pearl about them

SANGRE 24

A LEGACY

Grandfather never went to school
spoke only a few words of English,
a quiet man; when he talked
talked about simple things

planting corn or about the weather
sometimes about herding sheep as a child.
One day pointed to the four directions
taught me their names

El Norte

Poniente   Oriente

El Sur

He spoke their names as if they were
one of only a handful of things
a man needed to know

Now I look back
only two generations removed
realize I am nothing but a poor fool
who went to college

trying to find my way back
to the center of the world
where Grandfather stood
that day

Set in 12/13 Souvenir phototype and printed on 70 lb. Carnival ivory text by Roseta Press, Las Cruces, New Mexico. Cover is 65 lb. chestnut Teton cover with 80 lb. brown Teton text end papers. Cover photograph from *Leading Facts of New Mexico History*, Vol. II, 1912, The Torch Press. Design by Peter Kunz of San Francisco, California for **Prima Agua Press.** Printed in an edition of 1000, 50 of which are numbered and signed by the author.